LITERATURE AND LANGUAGE DEPARTMENT
THE CHICAGO PUBLIC LIBRARY
400 SOUTH STATE STREET
CHICAGO, ILLINOIS 60605

QUIVER

THE
VQR
POETRY
SERIES

Quiver

POEMS BY SUSAN B. A. SOMERS-WILLETT

The University of Georgia Press   *Athens & London*

Published by The University of Georgia Press
Athens, Georgia 30602
www.ugapress.org
© 2009 by Susan B. A. Somers-Willett
All rights reserved
Set in Garamond Premier Pro
Printed and bound by Thomson-Shore
The paper in this book meets the guidelines for
permanence and durability of the Committee on
Production Guidelines for Book Longevity of the
Council on Library Resources.

Printed in the United States of America

13 12 11 10 09 P 5 4 3 2 1

Library of Congress Cataloging-in-Publication Data

Somers-Willett, Susan B. A., 1973–
Quiver : poems / by Susan B. A. Somers-Willett.
        p.   cm. — (The VQR poetry series)
Includes bibliographical references.
ISBN-13: 978-0-8203-3327-4 (pbk. : alk. paper)
ISBN-10: 0-8203-3327-1 (pbk. : alk. paper)
I. Title.
PS3619.O445 Q58 2009
811'.6—dc22   2008048362

British Library Cataloging-in-Publication Data available

for Ernie
　　MY THEORY OF EVERYTHING

Contents

Acknowledgments *ix*

Quiver *1*

DARK MATTER: A LOVE STORY

Dark Matter: A Love Story *5*

A NATURAL ORDER

Relativity *15*

The Order of a House *17*

Darwin Strikes a Match *19*

The Golden Lesson *21*

SURVIVAL OF THE FITTEST

At Four a.m., She Is Reminded of Survival of the Fittest *27*

Weaving Qiviut *28*

Polaris *30*

Adaptation *32*

It Will Be a Moment Ordinary as This *33*

Everything from Shells *34*

My Natural History *37*

Cities of Amber, Cities of Stone *38*

Oppenheimer's Lament *40*

Proof *41*

The Living Chamber *43*

AVE

    Thaw and the Beginning of Everything   49

    Cotyledon   50

    First Sex   51

    Crossing Drosophila   53

    Campanology   54

    The Abandoned Garden   55

RADIUM MUSIC

    Radium: Serenade   59

    Love as an Aid to Hypothesis   60

    Half-Life   61

    Horses   62

    Automatic Writing   63

    Radium: Aubade   64

PRAISE

    Zero: A Meditation   67

    Winter Solstice at Thirty-Three   69

    The M in M-Theory   71

    Work   73

    The Anthropology of Gold   74

    Notes   77

Acknowledgments

Grateful acknowledgment is made to the journals and anthologies where the following poems first appeared, sometimes in earlier forms:

Gulf Coast: "Half-Life"
Indiana Review: "Radium: Serenade" and "Horses"
Iowa Review: "The Golden Lesson"
Painted Bride Quarterly: "Thaw and the Beginning of Everything"
Pebble Lake Review: "The Order of a House" and "Cotyledon"
Southern California Anthology: "Polaris"
Virginia Quarterly Review: "Darwin Strikes a Match," "First Sex," and "My Natural History"
West Branch: "Oppenheimer's Lament" and "Campanology"

"Polaris" won the 2005 *Southern California Anthology*'s Ann Stanford Poetry Prize. "Darwin Strikes a Match," "First Sex," and "My Natural History" won the *Virginia Quarterly Review*'s 2006 Emily Clark Balch Prize for Poetry.

I am greatly indebted to the Center for the Arts in Society at Carnegie Mellon University, the Alden B. Dow Center for Creativity, I-Park Artists' Enclave, the Andrew W. Mellon Foundation, and the Millay Colony for the Arts for their generous support during the completion of this book. To the staff members of these organizations, I thank you most especially for giving me and other working artists rooms of our own.

Deepest thanks to those who helped shape this book: Moira Muldoon, Farid Matuk, Anina Moore, Michelle Detorie, Genevieve Van Cleve, and Terrance Hayes. To Pat, Ernie, and Libby: Thank you for the gifts of your love and support.

QUIVER

It is clear that the choice of object that is one of the elements in the harmony of form must be decided only by a corresponding vibration in the human soul.

—WASSILY KANDINSKY

quiver. *v.* (1) to tremble with a small, rapid motion *n.* (1) a portable container for arrows (2) a collection or accumulation; an arsenal (3) in mathematics, an oriented graph of loops and arrows between vertices (see figure) (4) in physics, a diagram representing the matter content of a gauge theory that describes multidimensional objects used in string theory

THE JORDAN QUIVER

Quiver

A mathematician must ask of the equation
How best to draw what you yield.

In other words, will the numbers surrender
and be finite, tied forever to the path of this grid,

or will the directions of one's arrows be ignored.
Such are the brittle, illogical instructions of love.

If stumbling and blind, the archer Eros
had no clear target beyond what physics could explain,

thus making the success of his own affair
improbable. With no image for evidence,

he visited his lover only at night so that she too
could give no description of his horror or his heretofore

imaginary beauty. But here, among numbers,
the beloved is meant to rise, love's proof

like a queer mirror before me and saying *I do*.
In a quiver graph, all known objects connect—

points, lines, vertices, the ubiquitous loop
of Ouroboros consuming his tail.

Such is the beauty of the husband
drawing his path upon my body. Please.

Reckon to me this image. I have heard its splendor
will stay only briefly and is love's witness

running with its arms open all the way home.

Dark Matter: A Love Story

Dark Matter: A Love Story

The bright suns I see and the dark suns I cannot see are in their place.
—WALT WHITMAN

1

Listen. Hear as the night frog hears
with his lungs' fleshy tremor
the loose banjo string of his own throat.

For stars are born of such voices,
their parts held together by the gravity
of the vibrating dark,

darkness pressing and releasing a soft cage
on the pulsing systems of their hearts,

the resonant matter
of their atomic bodies oscillating
charcoal-dim to zither-bright.

Hear as the black vacuum hears
this song of hydrogen: her percussive body
strumming the sky's chemical bones.

Before the light of the world, such wild violins.

2

O lo, says Dark Matter
biting her nails in the pink
nursery of her sisters' birth—

a scowling teenager
sitting and darkly sitting
in the dull stellar glow
of their childish activity.
Here, she takes her slovenly
place in the family—

a dishrag, a fixture
no one notices with kindness;

sometimes she thinks they see her
not at all. In the background
of a white-trimmed photo,
she barely appears:

swarthy next to her shining blonde sisters

A little dark cloud they say

3

To wish to be spectacular

like an unlit match imagining to burn
or the spent match remembering its burning:
want flying over its pale wooden body
all acetylene brightness and rough sound—

a dense limb fearless
in knowing the flame, knowing its desire
equals its consumption,
use to uselessness in the motion
of a body made ash with abandon.

The matches in the fold-over book all agree
it is the most beautiful thing

4

He focuses his oversized spyglass to peer
into her sisters' windows at night.

He listens to their middling conversations
while diligently snapping photos
of their pointed, glowing breasts:

blooming pink nebulae, new womanliness
dissipating in the gossamer shifts
of their red nightgowns.

The stars vainly walk their corridor
playing prom queen late at night.
Dark Matter has been enlisted
to accompany each sharp-shifting sister
to her crowning and announcement
as a silent tuxedoed date.

The sisters trade the title between them
and with silver pins affix
their mother's old and brittle crown
worn like a planet's orbit.

It is then with his mirrors and sonar
that he comes to focus on her
  dark corona

5

  I am : you are
by the paths of the lights in the sky
moving away from the other
faster and faster in the subtle
    red shift—

      and it is in this space
that he wishes to touch her,
to press this deepening distance
like a soft mouth and shadow her
wine-dark body slipping between
the stars' sharp walls of light.

      By day : by night,
he listens to her talk alone in diffuse song

and she offers the whispered
lullaby of her black
and hissing tongue:

speech not cool
        like the trill of her mother's helium voice
but quietly hot
        like her body's burning done secretly and in the dark—

    6

      I love you

I love the brief wild eyes of you

I love the particle and wave of you
      the seen and unseen of you

I love you for I once was you and am still
the heart of your shine

    7

      She holds him in
this invisible quintessence

and although he knows what he cannot see
will destroy the stars' narrow paths,

he will still abandon his careful notes
on the distant stars for this song,

his elemental data shifting in the black
waves of the graph into her indefinite
shape into her sound—

his love a burning cluster:
        supernovae

his love collapsing in on itself

8

Her sisters grow thin
under the weight of her burden,

love's crushing gravity
obliterating the last of their lights—

    one of them grows dim and sullen
    turning red in the heart

    one of them explodes in anger

    one of them says nothing
    but is a giant gaping mouth

9

To be this invisible

like a man speaking into the black mouth
of a forest at night and receiving

no hard form in reply, the dark trees
offering him no dimension, no shape
meant to menace or welcome him in;

and so it is that you speak to me,
and so I know my black veil
of absence is my power. In you,

I become everything, or nothing, or instead
you hold your trembling hands in front of you
so that your hands can guess—

and in this moment of your eyeless search,
I can hear your body wondering
in the perfect dark;

in this world of your hands opening
and closing in on themselves with no proof

I can answer the distant circle
of your radio-weary voice—

10

At his burial there was no mention
of angelic resurrection
but there was a certain rising,
there was a certain carrying up:

not rising into the light,
  his soul lifting into it blissfully
  like a good spirit is always imagined to do
but dissipating into the dark,
  the secret matter of his heart becoming his body
  becoming his eyes becoming everything
  everywhere at once

11

And how urgent this message:

her dark pressing his light pressing his dark
bending over eons, each sent out in reply—

12

His bones, the pale light of his body diffusing
incandescent into all of her darkness like static—

striking once the match of his body
against the invisible air
and her love a listening:

      a voice burning in, burning out

13

And so too, this other music:

14

light reaching us after the light has gone out

A Natural Order

Relativity

If a man were to travel at the speed of light,
it is said he would return to find his son
an old man. The man would remain himself,
a petulant youngster amongst probing scientists,
or perhaps he would return as a clock-watching clerk
smoking at his desk in a patent office
and sipping a pungent coffee. Perhaps this man would return

to the woman he loved in the morning, make love
as the sun striates through pale lace curtains,
and perhaps in this world the word *love* means
I am gone, for what is presence but the slow
dancing of Mileva against the sheets?
Perhaps the word *love* means *elephants*
and the man's secret marriage is the slow lumbering
of an animal, a great gray machine.

If this man were to travel to the end
of the universe and back, perhaps
he could meet his son at the desk where he now sits,
time scratching its transparent name into record.
Perhaps his son would have sons, those close to the man's
own age, the moss on the grave of his wife
tatting a delicate lace. Today Mileva rests
her temples on her palms and sighs
in the black fabric of her dress,
the child making soft terrors in her belly.

be stricken in rain and drown in that music,
a bright water collecting and restless.
The queen delights in twisted wax and mud

and thrown-up paper and in winter
clips the drones' useless wings. There is nothing
they will not do for this woman. They make

their curious lives trying to make a voice with their wings,
and to stumblingly dance, and to dance ornately,
and to do as they are told all the way home

like you, the child who lived in this house,
or like the stuffed bear you wouldn't leave home without—
you buckled him in the backseat next to you,

his urgent gold plush worn to buds,
his misshapen head turned toward the window
as your mother drove you all over town.

Darwin Strikes a Match

Sweet tobacco wafts through the quarterdeck,
    around the sweating rungs and under the hatch,
while a perfumed woman schools the Captain
    to her wicked tattoos. She is rare
as a whale's tooth and as brown as she puffs
    a length of pipe and breathes it through
the pink interior of the Captain's room.
    Darwin sits quiet beside the Captain,
finishing the last of the swiveling port, the etched glass
    opening a crimson throat. The Captain's table
shines darkly, polished with wine revelers have slopped
    in salutation to the dawn and now this ash
that mists over the Captain's skylight so that
    there is no light but only fleck and spray.
For days the sailors wade through this smoke—
    the volcano on shore yielding slow fire
beyond the tree line—and the black water laps the ship
    with small tremors like the sick cat
lapping up the last of the wine. Having this woman
    onboard is unlucky, they know. Birds
have flown from the jungle. The lanterns and the table
    lean forward. The woman leans forward.
She is leaning to unbutton her shoes: no—
    she is picking up a fallen spoon. Her face
bends in the silver like a face of a coin distorts
    under a jeweler's loupe: a scratched and ill-lit glow.
She loosens her hair from a knot and lays her
    hands on the pocked wood of the table, on the smooth
candlelight that is the view of the table, her hair unraveling.
    Did the woman learn this from other travels,

or is this the sharp courtesy of a guest?
        Her hands fold, one small animal nesting into
another. It is almost evening now: the full lanterns up
              on bow and stern and all over this cramped town
that they live in, that they work with rotted braids of rope
                    and iron hooks through which the sailors string
the rot and sing. Her hands are quiet specimens
          on the table as Darwin bends down and lifts
the hoop, her petticoat and its crisp waves receding
             in her grasp. *The leg is beyond repair*, Darwin says
to the Captain, and so it is. They lift her to half-standing,
             they give her the feast of old bread and hard
cheese and the wine in which there swirls dirt, and the swain
              is calling, the swain is calling, the fire made rain
falls over them like a muslin cloth—little room to breathe
           in the hothouse—and they toss and toss
as Darwin returns to his torrid chamber
              and is sick in the corner: it is his name for the storm
and it is his name for the woman now fanning
            her face with a small dirty plate.
Come morning, the sailors will throw anchor and row
            their cargo to the village, the woman
cursing against the plume of her skirt trailing
            in the brackish water: its black uneven weight.
They will stretch her good leg gently, as if
              stretched to collect rain, all the while the woman
looking to the ash-ridden sky saying
           Dígame, Dígame, Dígame.

The Golden Lesson

Leonardo cracks the thief's sternum with precision
and opens the body's proportion, fearful symmetry
glistening in the flat wet lungs like a bird's folded wings

or two lozenges of yellow amber laid on a plate.
He licks his fingertips blackened by thin strips of kohl
as the cat suddenly and impolitely asks for its dinner.
A body does not do as it is told. He has called Giacomo in,
but the boy is rudely eating a wedge of pink melon

in the kitchen. Sucking at it, in fact. So that
his hands will stick with the fruit all night and
the pages of his books will bear stains and his boyish odor.

The gray shade of evening falls over corpse and artist
as a candle flickers against the body's dark ruin,
the neck corded with hard tendon to tether
the shoulder's weight of brain and skull and through it all
the windpipe ridged with cartilage climbing up

like a soft ladder into the palate. The boy
and his seventeen years know nothing of this,
the life dissected and sectioned out into a dark oval,

which is the head, which leans back as if on a string
tied to the throat; so that the throat opens
into a white-stringed harp centering the imaginary
line between halves of the body, the sketch nearly ready
but for one criminal eye looking up to the artist from the table,

removed from the patient with such desire like seeking
a stray precious marble. Leonardo calls the boy Salai,
which means demon. He pulls back the curtain

to reprimand the malingering boy who
now has anise candy on his breath, and although
he knows Salai has stolen to have it,
he does not comment because the licorice seed
sweetens the room. The thief's hands cripple

on the wood table, and the boy wonders
what pleasure was held in this criminal wrist—perhaps
a thirst made its way into the body to play these strings

and the tongue and hand answered. Salai skims
the corpse's dull skin with his finger, the body
pinned down by the puckering O of the navel,
his hand almost free of youth's dimension.
The criminal eye does nothing

but hold vigil in its rind of boiled egg white
like a blue jewel encrusting a pale woman's ear.
Perhaps the eye will study the artist

as he draws the body. Perhaps, inside the eye,
an inverted picture of the two scholars will glint
as they point and argue about man's divine proportion
and in their conversation will rise a sound from the thief
like a harsh note forbidden in the box of a guitar:

the imperfect soul made art from the Orphic
instrument of muscle and calcium set ringing: yes:
in this room with the blackening window

and the organs' sweet odor hotly releasing,
the criminal will speak the feckless boy and his teacher
like a dark chorus and the indivisible golden chord
will fly up. And who will hear this joy of the body?
Who will play the harp in the boy?

Survival of the Fittest

At Four a.m., She Is Reminded of Survival of the Fittest

That was when she awoke to find a doe
peering at her in the total dark, the animal's
sharp, wondering head thrust through the open
window and gazing at her still as sculpture.
This was the doe's quiet address. Then:
a sound like small human crying in the tall
black weeds. She dressed and found it with a flashlight.
When it cried, it showed a pointy pale tongue
and its wide, speckled belly was taut as a thumb.
The doe circled it for some time, nosing
its white-tipped rear until the fawn folded
onto its side and could do nothing
but cry distress. Hours passed as the doe paced
and sniffed the rank air. And then, *like that*,
the doe turned and loped off stonily
into the shocking pink crepe myrtle,
her hooves listing soundlessly in dust.
And so, the sick fawn kept calling
into the summer day. Even now,
my friend sometimes hears a child wear
the dress of its voice. She called to see
what to do with it. And so. We wrapped it
in a cape of dull green plastic. Something
made for trash. I remember its eyes
bending light into its small body. We did it together,
arriving in silence at the arid edge of town. No,
we did not name it. Nor did we bury it, but left it
to the hawks and the dogs and the rain.

Weaving Qiviut

When they feed, do the oxen
      reason with the tough grass
           and know that they were missed?
      Do they carry in their bodies memory
of the tundra's firmness,
      of the sharp, salted trees
           against which they sharpen
their dark commas of horn?
They mate on the grounds
      where they were hunted. A mother
           introduces her steaming calf to the plain,
a quick stab of ice in her lungs.
Will the weaver render this desire
      into song? Will her fabric whisper,

      Keep safe, for some
      will survive even you?

After all, it is about holes
      and how one moves between them.
           The shuttle fits neat in the lap
      of the weaver before she thrusts
its rough body through the ox wool.
      Persistence, she says, skimming her cracked
           Alaskan hands over the nachaq
      and pushing through the tool.

This is the art of resurrection:
>	the musk ox once extinct here and
>>	later shipped in from another country
>	in a boat packed with tiny braying.

Calves were created like the weave—
>	partly by will, partly by design—and so
>>	the oxen experience a planned love.
>	From women's looms evolve

a dancer's furious legs, pulsing urchins,
>	seal hunters that forever circle
>>	a scarf's soft hole of ice and wait
>	for prey to take the oily bait.

Dark forms on snow,
>	you do what the living do:
>>	remembering not the weaver
>	but the design, the snow a shroud

falling over this morning's
>	trees and their greening.

Polaris

Along the wooden tourist bridge
sockeye salmon thrash their way upriver,
throwing their sperm to the current
in tiny white cords, and we snicker
at the brutishness of it all, the bruised pink males
looking for love in all the wrong places.

In these protein cords lies a burning science,
a study of motion. Translucent heads shiver
like their fish fathers struggling
against the river's cold form:
a mirror held to the large and small.
The inefficient business of male and female
halves meeting with haphazard purpose.
Or not meeting, the body whispering desperation
in its skin. The sun barely sets
during this season—even midnight
brings a shallow light—
and so it is under this eye

that sperm burrow hot
into a blushing pocket of red roe,
both glad to be found if only
for the finding, blooming sometimes
over and sometimes under and sometimes
only the two electric things pulling
fruitlessly away from each other

like a poor fisher
trying to reel in a struggler with a bum hook,
or the Earth spinning away from its nights,
or the way we will love each other
today or the next day or the next.

Adaptation
SEPTEMBER 2002

In the heart of Manhattan, a black bear
strips the flesh from a branch and chews it through,
pensively, behind velvet rope. Lucy views
her audience, desperate, her monkeyish hair
innocent in the busy museum, ash where
fire has tested her bones to glass. Fortitude,
Darwin said, is innate to species, true—
but trauma is a badge she'd rather fear than bear.

I know this like a mare knows to lick her foal
or a peahen knows her mate's ceaseless angling;
even worms shrink from light despite their lack
of eyes. In the Ocean Hall, squid and whale roll
maw to maw toward the grim-toothed fish dangling
his lure to a child, all of us ready for attack.

It Will Be a Moment Ordinary as This

walking with him in the hard-lit grocery　　　when you realize
　　among the announcements and　　turning a corner down aisle three
　　　　that you have taken him　　yes you have
　　　　　　taken him　　with your hips　　hitting the note of
the metal grocery basket　　there between the flesh
　　　of pasta and stuffed olives　　pressed against glass to see
　　　　　　　　the bright noose
　　of his love take shape　　and engirth

the rest of his days in suddenly　　and when suddenly
　　comes years later　　a slight shifting in your sleep
　　　　　keeps him awake　　and here too the messy house and the terror
of broken china　　which is your accidental anger
　　　　and whose sound surprises even you　　as it satisfies

　　the dish　　its sharp crescent a relief　　a gift
　　　　　　　from your family's women
　　　　　on its face splays a dull brown peahen　　riffling
through the scrape of a thousand meals　　and which warms
　　　　now to hear　　her mate's ragged horn piercing the rim

what now will you do with his song of want
　　　will you make a life of it

Everything from Shells
E Conchis Omnia, DARWIN FAMILY MOTTO

Husbands and wives settle in the oddest
        of places, some of them only
copying themselves selfishly, folding over and
        creating no variety, some of them
gluing themselves head to head in marriage.
        For years the stalked barnacles have eaten
a mottled triton under Darwin's watch,
        their homes made in the glossy
ivory furrows after cunningly evicting their host
        and the fleshy conch left searching
for another shell like a lost, off-color tongue
        gently slapping the sea floor.
Sometimes Darwin speaks to the barnacles.
        Sometimes he calls his children in for a lesson
and focuses the scope and steadies the glass plate,
        for in each mating and repeating species
sealed meticulously between asphalt and glass
        twists the ghost of Darwin's daughter.
Today the barnacles are reproducing and dying,
        reproducing and dying, and through
the white slough of bodies, the females spread
        their umbrellas of pink feather and bone
to catch the young and the dead and embrace both
        in a simple mouth. He thinks of
Annie seized over in a tubercular cough
        as he observes them strain to collect

  the floating matter, each opening to the other,
    the anchored bodies translucent models
of spine and grace and the children slipping through
    their mothers' grasps to prove the theory:
the strongest slip though. His study is dizzy
  with the saccharine odor of brandy
as he opens the jars of barnacles and
    drains them of preserving spirits
and dissects each structure with steel pins. The parasitic
    males pry their way in—tiny sacs
embroidering their women's bodies with code—
    and thus fixed and half-embedded
in the flesh of their wives they pass
    the whole of their lives immobile.
Across the table, a jar of orange coral
    retracts into stone as a family
of pinned beetles reflect light with their
    sable armor. Some mornings
Darwin takes his sons hunting and the retriever
    trots over the hill with a glossy-eyed fowl
draped in the soft grip of its mouth.
    Some mornings his daughter, like a mirror,
rises in the study among the specimens:
    these floating lives preserved
in the work of the world and the work
    of the body precious. She is copied
now as the breathing cellulose of a weed
    ruffles before a gas lamp, or now
as the yellowing leaf outside his window
    shines translucent and golden in the

sudden brief afternoon light and after
   seasons of opening to it—after belief
unfurled each day in its bright pointed face—
   this wind, and a quiet letting go. The gentle
father bores in deeper. He will cling to this girl
   like a jellyfish wraps its bell
around a darling fish to keep it:
   he will cling to her like the best shell.

My Natural History

This is how my father will tell it:
he is a young man, not even twenty,
driving down a road in Arizona with my mother
and searching for the place where they will park,
put their backs to cool June grass,
and lie naked together for the first time.
In his mind he is also another man:
one in the last few weeks of his dying,
and in his end he finds himself wondering
over their naked bodies in the field from above
as broken aloe weeps a sharp green perfume.
He marvels at the geography of her brown hair,
the order of her fingers in moonlight like thin
lit stones. He feels the first tremor, sees himself
shift over, begins again in the rift
of red stone that opens between them.
The rocks push through layers of sediment and he
crosses the pale borders of shale plates and limbs,
a mountain rising in her hip and his future
spiraling in a fossil of white shell. The water
is rising up to run its dark course:
the water will wear her form for years.
As the gap yawns wider, it is this history
he chooses to remember:
a young woman, not even twenty,
reclining in the grass and the distance.
The blade of a river flowing between them
in which their daughter is being carried away.

Cities of Amber, Cities of Stone

Cast softly in a sea of wing and bone,
some of them glow in small moments:

a termite working its dark knot of wood,
a scissor-jawed ant innocently chewing a bough

of weeping acacia—the body overtaken
in the quotidian and now attending its own memorial

as if presented with a sudden exam.
Some knew the struggle useless, and so,

like the human fossils at Pompeii,
they cradle things dear: a twig or favorite shell,

swift darling prey; even the acid-
mouthed spider folds his legs like an ancient

card table and clutches his own belly for comfort.
Others mug for posterity, gesturing Shakespearean

in their graves. A damselfly drifts up
on the Baltic shore in a rough green cabochon,

her detached wing floating above her
like a last breath or a bubble of speech.

In that moment, stuck fast, her spiracles
beat hot like a gun firing in the body,

tomorrow, tomorrow, I know.
She breaks like those drowning

in attics, precious wrecks, the torn
and open wing like the ribs

of a house hacked through
to the sky. I know you, face of faces,

bloated by sap and open water.
I watch your eyes happening in the glass.

Oppenheimer's Lament

Like a good doctor, I am meant to wean
the thing from the love of its mother—
I will burn it, I will make it clean—

careful speed forced between
the patient poles, one circling the other
like a good doctor. I am meant to wean

strong from weak, and in the break, the seam
of fire pulls from its awful cover.
I will burn it, I will. Make it clean,

this break: let the cloven atom shine in tourmaline
brilliance until brilliance is over.
Like a good doctor, I am meant to wean

my hand from its only career, my heart lean
as we cross the incandescent desert together.
I will burn it. I will make it clean

as a glass bowl, and the cracked globe will gleam—
for in this moment, the world has no tether.
A good doctor, I am meant to wean.
I will burn it. I will make it clean.

Proof
AFTER SCHRÖDINGER'S THOUGHT EXPERIMENT

Look. The cat, for all its pink-lunged mewing,
is ultimately not the important thing. Neither is the vial,

nor its terrible-sounding poison; even the rogue atom
and its elaborate mechanism to crack the vial's glass

is distraction from the real point, its radioactive body
glowing threateningly bright. In fact, you could imagine the cat

to be an exotic bird, or a childhood friend, or a favorite
novel or loud spot by the sea. Or this: your father's

hard-won embrace, that fling in Barbados, blackberries
shining like dark eyes in the salad, or the first time you saw

her small, freckled breasts resting in the pale sling
of morning light. The cat makes no difference. Any of these

other things will do. Now, imagine this thing
in the clutch of danger. Imagine that despite the experiment's rigor

there is no way of knowing in any given hour whether
it lives or dies. Instead, you must entertain the notion

that your beloved is dead, or is living blissfully
unaware of your worry, frying morning eggs and bacon

in an apartment at some unknown address. Then,
the whole of your time is spent inventing stories

that end in interminable suspense: *maybe, it's
plausible, probably this and assumedly that*. . . .

In this dark sky of the mind there winks
no sign, and so fear and wild possibility.

For example, when posed with the question
Do you love me or do you not love me?

he answers, *Yes*. That is all
one can say to such wayfaring danger.

That is all the soldier can offer the quick
gun-wielding boy in his sight.

The Living Chamber

1. The Shell

For the love of the word. For the love of the world.

For the love of the world he knows my brother says
the word sputteringly as he sweating drags

the body heavy in his arms his breath exploding
his knees exploding his teeth exploding with this weight

his muscles ribboning in his shoulder's skin until
he releases the body into an oiled mouth ogive end down

O give him this black quiet
moment here still in the row as the shell

sleeps breathing its peaceful inanimate metal sleep
his blighted hands disagreeing with the fuse and then

the machine with his hands made alive into this voice

2. Shells

To mark the years a nautilus seals off a chamber of its
shell with secretions that become the thin iridescent rungs of

the interior this is what the skin of the animal gives to build
a fire deep in the sand its twisted minaret glowing to tell

the body's history in shape in shell it opens
into the living chamber which is the dark office

of the weary nautilus retreating from the mouth
of the world so to sleep under its hood or to wring

its prey in the absence of light it is the room
where the creature comes to rest like a fist to ponder

the days of its fierce joy and discontent

3. The Shells

the desert
is glittering with the small jewels of fires and

people raving
with their arms upraised do the acetylene cars give praise

this morning
do they hear their names as the pressure drops inside

a boiling ear where
does the soul live is it here in this boy in his beauty

as he clicks
to illuminate and explode does his mother

know love
as it screams or sails effortlessly to enter her

shattered window
and translate her face into a great broken

mouth hinged
toward heaven this poem too lives in the mouth and speaks

as the soldier's
gun speaks *forgive* the simple flesh parting

4. Birthday

The weather is reading your body tonight is announcing
storms even the dog cowers as the new evening parts

a slit of blue a vein in the pale cloud of sky it bulges soft
Braille your body a cloud the water asleep but distantly rumbling

thunder a sudden incision of sound of muffled conflict
of hands clapping their joyful commands into what

we are all delivered one room and then another
one room this year of war and how we are married to it how

with wet hands we fumble and slip into the dark shell
of house shaking our pitiful umbrellas and cursing

the half-sheathed newspaper melting on the step this
is how the doctor reads your woman's body in pieces and with hands

reading the percussion above beneath the heavy sluice and
through it listen to the rain's report insisting on the tin porch roof

listen to the sky protest as it delivers this room of brief light

Ave

Thaw and the Beginning of Everything

The monk crosses the garden's grassy islands of ice
balancing a vaporing cup of tea on a bone saucer.
He is singing matins in the plot.
He fingers the toughened peas in his pocket.
Their thin, brittle coats diminish,
evaporating in his hands
like onion skin or flakes of gold paper.

They have been waiting, patient
as the Earth is patient in its hours
for the day. And now, above the garden,
brothers lay down their gilded books
on angled tables to watch Gregor
break the gray crust of the garden
with a spade. And now *Ave*.
And now the votive's glow in red glass.
And now dawn's aureole peeping
around his soutane bringing light,
more perilous, interrupting light.
This is how silently he breaks the world.

Cotyledon

I split to reveal a white tongue.
It screws into the earth to root
like a spike driven through wax
by an invisible hammer.
In the dark nests of clover, I shiver
a limb with two upturned leaves.
These leaves are my palms asking.
This opening is the sound of my voice.

First Sex

Who would guess that glory
would live on a pea plant's
sticky mouth smeared

with golden pollen?
The monk frees
the flowers' sexes

from calico bonnets
and shoos the abbot's
sweet-bottomed bees

and with tweezers snips
powder from the anthers
while the style hot with nectar

reaches up. He pushes the tip
of the camel-hair brush
in this bright dust—

and the bells of the flowers
twist to him; the knotting tendrils
strain on their brittle twigs—

and the tiny stem is painted
gently, as if it were
a thread of spun glass.

The opening yellow
bud swallows
the scientist's bait

and it floats down
into the ovum like a
point of light in the throat

so that the whole body
is singing deep praise
of his touch and oh

yes Mendel this
moment is the best
of glory's evidence—

one can see it even
in the white blossom's
effusion of bliss.

Crossing Drosophila

Translucent larvae bloom in the dish
as the stern-faced teacher
sorts the virgins by sex

I shroud their stunned bodies with the sleep box
I douse the cotton with a dropper
            my youth sings the ether

What feral curiosity drives these children
to shake the specimens and rap the glass?

       (power moving over them
            like a rough and heavy brocade)

I know the beauty of your torture
O child of Mengele, O Sierra Leone

O bright, wingless daughter

O wild, red-eyed thing

Campanology

The black crow righteously grips the fence while
the staccato of rain fills the pea blossoms' adolescent boats

to play like bone dice in a cup. Later, the collector
will gather them up, a lone bee ringing that word

behind him, *lust*, whatever it was this garden used to render.
For they wish to be shrill as a chorus of eunuchs, purple and white lips

pursed against entry and the stamens clipped to lend
chastened blooms. And so their answer to desire is closure.

And so the perfume of the body becomes the green
song of their palms thrilling in the wind.

This afternoon, Mendel naps in his humid cell,
his shrugging penis curling fatly into his innocent thigh,

while across the field, the rose bush casts its scent
like a dark meat over the city, black pungent silks folding

and folding back into a crown of soft decay. And so
in the heart of the rose is a knelling. And so in the bloom

is a call to music, tongues ululating in want,
and the sound in the garden is youth

beating out its name like an anthem,
like rain on the body of a bell.

The Abandoned Garden

You could say that we went wild.
Our breeds left to cross and tangle
in the absence of Mendel's collection.
Like his school children respectfully
bequeathing him parting gifts and then
running breathlessly toward summer
at the sound of the year's final
bell. Or like a bird whose cage door
has opened, a bird who is deciding
whether or not it should flee
and then flees.

Radium Music

Radium: Serenade

Initially, Pierre thinks women a distraction. Distracting, yes—
he bends from his work to imagine their gross imprecision
and perilous hair. His small basement lab sweats the Seine into air,

altering moments of small magnetism as they pass

through the gap of his instrument. The careening needle at the center
is never meant to pierce or mend, but it is,
at a certain temperature, electric.

Marie enters marriage as if stepping into a lead box.

The first X-ray published was of Frau Röntgen's left hand
laid on a photographic plate, ghostly articulations of bone
circled by the black halo of her wedding ring.

The hand opens as if to say hello, exhibiting,
among other things, its safety.

In this manner, Marie would later capture a nail in a boy's lung,
a horse's skull, a soldier's hip shattered by a bullet in the field.

The public took these images to be premonitions of death,
or worse: a sight into the inviolable body, which is the domain of God.

In Greek, the word *atom* means *indivisible*, as in *not to cut*.

Night falls so that light is in reverse, shining
to glow in a room where lovers vow their bodies to discovery.

This night I hold a candle to the body's negative
and see through it in shapes of light.

Love as an Aid to Hypothesis

If pitchblende is placed between four charged plates
then one may measure its weight by the balance

waving its dull light on the wall.
If the element is radioactive, then it will

illuminate the new husband down to his gentle bones.
He will not know it, but such work will make his body

open as the field in Brittany in which he and Marie
first make love, tumors softly knuckling

in his side, in her side, exposed. In the lab,
they figure their question into fact:

If and only if to marry is to surrender
one's parts to the other, then his body

will adore and adore her painfully
in its guess. The body repeats itself

in sickness, in health. This morphology
of danger is their making.

The radon gas under glass clouds over.
From him, she will never recover.

Half-Life

A thing in itself always diminishes. From this:

light, heat, the order of matter burning into more matter.

The radium atom in particular proves unstable and thus produces tiny blue lights, which is not unlike a view of the world from above in satellite. In the damp laboratory at night, and for their enjoyment, Pierre and Marie dance among ramshackle benches and glowing bulbs of glass. Flame stutters: a question in the lamp.

Their fingers soon turn black with the burns of their work.

In this they know that what they study is the chemistry of perdition.

That the source of the light in the world is the world's demise.

Marie figures the days left of its hazard and its blessing.

Horses

In yet another summer of Russian regret, Marie's father fed apples to the soldiers' horses. *No need for the servants of tyrants to suffer*, he said before approaching them and peering into the world of their black and uniformed eyes. Marie, at the curb, could not see behind the blind, but she could imagine the horse's wild pupil floating there behind the stiff, black disk, her humble afternoon filling with the scent of sour hay and new leather. Thinking of them that evening, she grew afraid of the mare's teeth, living as they do in the mouth, rein and strop falling away to deliver noise and unseen purpose. Years later, Pierre distractedly crosses the Rue Dauphine in fat rain and is struck by a dray. Some say his mind was off and thinking of Marie. Some say it was the umbrella held to the globe of his head as a black shield from the rain. The rain: the hoof: its quick: the strike: the light: a shroud: the black of the shield. The horses of her childhood did not eat kindly, but tore the whole small globe of the apple out of her father's hand. In this she learned the division of parts. Even the beloved atom sings harm in its loss.

Automatic Writing

Dearly departed, for if there is a link between radioactivity and the spirit, I will find it.

Dearly departed, for I will find it, for I will let its word pass across my daughters and work.

Dearly departed, for the word of morning and its white hour caused you to depart, and for that, the last words I said to you were cross words.

Dearly departed, for you crossed the doorway into the open mouth of day.

Dearly departed: the traffic of horses in rain.

Dearly departed, which is to say interrupted by death.

Dearly departed, for I remember the evening we watched a gram of radium burn in the parlor, and your face became a specter's in its light.

Dearly departed, for belief wears my flesh like a wife.

Dearly departed, the X in X-ray stands for the unknown.

Radium: Aubade

Now all of Paris begs
to tremble in my
artificial light,
the bellies of pianos
churning their
fin de siècle blues—

I am pressed
to a woman's ailing
temple and like
the city, I incandesce.

What could I give
these two who burned
a ton of earth to an atom
and who so perilously shook
the glass in which my
blue light shon?

With such ostentation, I pass
into them and through
the body of the world
playing my eighty-eight
keys to prove it.

I open my mouth
to crow
the dawn atomic.

Praise

Zero: A Meditation

Ending : an endlessness

the spaceman floating in a chlorinated pool
and his wild radioed ascent

hard start : silence in the copse
as the panting dog arrives to point

his son was laid to rest on a Monday

emptiness impossible
to divide or divide by

it wings into the vanishing
point of a Dührer landscape

the weightless body of a young brown owl in the palm

beginning and end : rain
in the crying pines

infinite : void; affirmation : negation

the obliterating circle of green chile
tossed in the soup at Kang's

— O —

the place-holding
jacket laid across a velvet auditorium seat

beautiful archipelago
of a dead man's dress shoes in the closet

    —and yet I whisper
into the pores of this blank canvas

it is said she knows
how to clear a room well

Winter Solstice at Thirty-Three

And still. And still the involute symmetry
of a globe of cabbage flowering on its ivory stalk,

nodes of kale swirling like dark, elaborate
birds in snow. This rusty pinhole moon also

knows the order of its sides, dimly walking
the narrow window of its orbit by day

like a pale cloistered girl, faces visible
and invisible, closing surely as an eye closes

for sleep and pulling its slow black lid
over everything, its shroud falling over my body.

Tonight the light of the sky declines.
Tonight the last palms of lilies applaud

in black praise on the silver-backed pond,
clustered in a shock of frost like a dark

pupil floating hard in a human eye and
shrinking as the ice makes time,

the plant and the frost branching
away from the other in scrolls of trauma,

one half-finished and the other half-begun.
Under my knife, a spotted trout opens to bloom

like a quivering pink flower, and this too
is praise: its river-soaked mouth snaps

in air to leave the dark and aqueous half
of his world. The slick-backed beaver

slaps her tail on her den in report. And so,
I am ending. And so I am beginning again.

The M in M-Theory

may stand for *membrane*, or *matrix*,
or if considered in the slanting light of days

that seem to sing everything, the light moving
strong and white from behind the brief

shadow of a cloud and into the room where you
have just made love, and it falls on your body and fills

your organs like gospel, your body still
but something inside whispering like a bird

settling its wings in the rain—then the M
might suggest *metaphysical, magic, mystery*,

the character with its mitered joints joining
your body, the room, this language

of simple light and bones. The scientists themselves
could not agree on the precise meaning and so now

math enacts speculation, theory's shadow
growing larger across the wandering stairs

of the mind like a mother peering in
on her sleeping child and receiving the blank,

open face of his dream in reply. This afternoon
you think the M is for *man, muscle, magnetic, make,*

but perhaps in this universe of complements
the M is also meant to suggest its inverse,

the W, which is the V doubled upon itself,
and here suddenly is the world waking

to look at its face repeating in that weird field
of glass, recto and verso, the symmetrical mouth

of a rose exploding in its desire to sing
the original mystery, the brief and unspeakable

name written and slipped between the ribs
of a clay monster, so that the monster comes

alive, so that this monster begs to hum
its rude praise for the rose, its damp red

throat opening in what tremolo.

Work

Like the pearly grubs that inch underground
or potato bugs curling in daylight,
their armor arched to protect ripe bellies
and then soft retreating;

like the threat of darkened street corners
or a scarecrow's black crown of birds;

like the long breath leaving the mouths of dead
and also living's beginning: exit;

like the light of things that are made hollow;

like the quick fish who vibrate in seaweed and are gone,
fish that plummet and surface and arc brilliant in sun
and then think nothing of eating one another—
        a deep chain;

as letters sent and which receive no reply;
as the comedy that brings no laughter;
as the egg-white eyes of a sightless man wandering
across a face with no purpose;

like animals violating the grass; so

we know the valley. We know the steep
walk of the hill. And still your palm knows
its praise of the world, whispering
its old human oil across my shoulders,

lightly cupping the two caps of bone
before returning to its blind
and many-veined work.

The Anthropology of Gold

Because the whole world is made of it;
because it is the world's first word
written on a gilded scroll unfurling
out of the lion's jaw. Its brief phrase

is in us just as it is in this yellow animal
playing the soft rare bones of prey
in his mouth: *Gloria Mundi*, desire
like a muscled cloud spilling out

of the elk's staunch breast. This morning,
I reach stone deep in the garden
and think of the believing alchemist
burying his rank vessel into the fire,

for years blindly expecting his wealth
to appear, *something from nothing*, his ear foolishly
pressed to the crucible listening for
the thin drawl of gold to rise from the bowl—

and I too wish for it, this preciousness—
and I too think to see it
in the river's flash of afternoon riches,
or in the marksman's bright arrow

purring in its slot, or in the brief slanting light
pouring through the skin of orange lilies like a breath.
Today, for example, I find a bee alive
and innocently dancing in the dog's mouth.

To speak the rare code of this world,
I will toil endlessly over its gifts
knowing it would yield
such incongruous treasure.

So that I could bite down,
hard. So that I could hold
all my love for the world
between my simple teeth.

Notes

Dark Matter: A Love Story

Recent theories have suggested that space is not composed of an empty vacuum, but that it is instead filled with an invisible substance called "dark matter"—also called "dark energy" or "quintessence"—that exerts a miniscule amount of gravity upon stars and other heavenly bodies. Although exactly what comprises dark matter remains a mystery, some scientists have postulated that is it most likely made of heretofore unseen subatomic particles vibrating in and out of existence.

Of course, such particles are impossible to observe accurately, as Werner Heisenberg put forth in his uncertainty principle of 1926: the nature of subatomic particles' speed and position is fundamentally changed by the mere act of observation, making a visual model of the atom obsolete. Heisenberg instead favored a mathematical model of the atom, which calculated the *probability* of the speed and position of subatomic particles within the atom, but which, because it was based in statistics, forced scientists to entertain the possibility of subatomic matter existing everywhere at once. This probabilistic model is widely accepted today.

As the visual model of the atom fell out of favor, some astronomers turned to radio waves to study the nature of space and elemental matter. Arno Penzias and Robert Wilson were one such pair of researchers, albeit unwittingly. In 1965, they were trying to make use of a large communications antenna in Holmdel, New Jersey, owned by Bell Laboratories, but their data were skewed by a faint and steady hiss in the background. After trying to eliminate the hiss with no success (including scrubbing out bird excrement from the receiving dish), Penzias and Wilson called Robert Dicke at Princeton University to ask for his assistance. Dicke realized immediately what the other two scientists had not, that the hiss was the earliest evidence of the Big Bang—ancient cosmic radiation that over time and distance had been converted into microwaves.

Weaving Qiviut

The musk ox, once indigenous to Alaska, was hunted to extinction in the 1850s. In the 1930s, the oxen were reintroduced by man to the area and, one hundred years after their extinction, they were farmed and domesticated for their special brand of wool known as qiviut. Today the qiviut is spun, woven, and knitted into signature patterns by native Alaskan women who are members of a musk ox cooperative. *Nachaq* is an Eskimo word for hood.

Everything from Shells

At the same time that Charles Darwin studied barnacles he had collected during his voyage on the *Beagle*, his eldest and favorite daughter, Annie, fell ill and died at age ten of tuberculosis. Understanding the importance of genetic variety for survival, he blamed himself for his daughter's illness; he believed that marrying his first cousin, Emma, had produced a sickly child. Annie's death has been considered by many as the ultimate reason why Darwin renounced his religious beliefs.

The description in this poem of the male barnacle's habits is derived from a note in one of Darwin's notebooks: "larvae become parasitic within the sack of the female, & thus fixed & half embedded in the flesh of their wives they pass their whole lives and can never move again."

Erasmus Darwin, Charles Darwin's naturalist grandfather, who first put forth the idea that all living organisms were descended from microscopic sea creatures, designed a family crest bearing the motto *E Conchis Omnia*: "Everything from Shells."

Proof

To illustrate the indeterminacy of quantum physics, Austrian physicist Erwin Schrödinger devised a now-famous thought experiment. A hypothetical cat is placed inside a box with a vial of hydrocyanic acid attached to a mechanism containing a single atom of radioactive material. If, within the course of an hour, the atom decays, the mechanism breaks the vial and the acid is released, killing the cat. If the atom does not decay, the vial remains intact and the cat lives. Because one cannot observe what actually happens inside the box, Schrödinger stipulated that one would have to regard the cat's existence in terms of probability, as both 100 percent living and 100 percent dead simultaneously. He used this elaborate example to show that what appears patently absurd in our world—that something could be both wholly living and dead—could be true in the quantum world, where the state of matter is determined by probability rather than observation.

Radium Music

Marie and Pierre Curie, who spent their lives studying the nature of radioactivity, met while Pierre was conducting studies on piezoelectricity at the Sorbonne. They married and worked together to discover a number of radioactive elements, including radium in 1898.

Initially, the Curies did not know of the detrimental effects radioactivity could have on the body and worked for many years with no protection from the harmful rays. Ever fascinated with potential links between spirituality and science, they reportedly attended séances with radium in hand. Such exposure took its toll on the health of the Curie family. Pierre showed signs of bone degeneration before his accidental death in 1906, when he was crushed by a horse-drawn carriage while crossing the Rue Dauphine during a rainstorm. Marie died of anemia related to exposure. Their daughter Irène Joliot-Curie, who continued her parents' research after their deaths, died of leukemia. Marie was so grieved by her husband's death that, for a year following his demise, she addressed her diary directly to Pierre's spirit.

Both Marie and Irène were pioneers in using radioactivity for medical purposes. During World War I, the mother and daughter operated mobile X-ray units, nicknamed *petites Curies*, aiding greatly in the treatment of French soldiers wounded in the field.

Radium's atomic number is eighty-eight, the same number as a piano has keys.

The M in M-Theory

M-theory is a proposed theory in physics that connects five different types of string theory through dualities, a series of mathematical relationships that allows one type of theory to translate to another. It is suggested by some to be the gateway to "the theory of everything"—a theory that explains all physical phenomena. M-theory was developed by mathematical physicist Edward Witten, who himself did not designate what the "M" signified. He suggested several possibilities, including "mystery," "matrix," or "magic," and others have suggested it stands for "the mother of all theories." Still others have suggested that the M is an inverted W meant to indicate Witten himself. M-theory, like string theory, is still being researched, and it is not without skeptics.

The Anthropology of Gold

In pursuit of the philosopher's stone, a substance that was fabled to transform base metals into gold, alchemists of the sixteenth and seventeenth centuries produced instructional texts complete with engravings depicting chemical processes. However, as they wished these processes to remain veiled to the general public, the texts employed elaborate pictorial codes and allegories. For example, a lion devouring prey might represent the strength of an acid or perhaps the union of two elements. *Gloria Mundi*, or *Glory of the World*, is the title of one such sixteenth-century alchemical text.

THE

POETRY SERIES

The VQR Poetry Series strives to publish some of the freshest, most accomplished poetry being written today. The series gathers a group of diverse poets committed to using intensely focused language to affect the way that readers see the world. A poem, at its heart, is a statement of refusal to accept common knowledge and the status quo. By studying the world for themselves, these poets illuminate what we, as a culture, may learn from close inspection.

SERIES EDITOR
Ted Genoways

VQR POETRY BOARD
David Lee Rubin, Chair
John Casteen
Jennifer Chang
Angie Hogan
Walt Hunter
Karen Kevorkian
Julia Kudravetz
Jon Schneider

BOOKS IN THE SERIES

The History of Anonymity
Jennifer Chang

Hardscrabble
Kevin McFadden

Field Folly Snow
Cecily Parks

Boy
Patrick Phillips

Salvinia Molesta
Victoria Chang

Anna, Washing
Ted Genoways

Free Union
John Casteen

Quiver
Susan B. A. Somers-Willett